NANUET PUBLIC LIBRARY

W9-BCY-080

J
599.79
Hew   Hewett, Joan

           A harbor seal pup
           grows up

                          $ 21.95

DUE DATE

NANUET
PUBLIC
LIBRARY

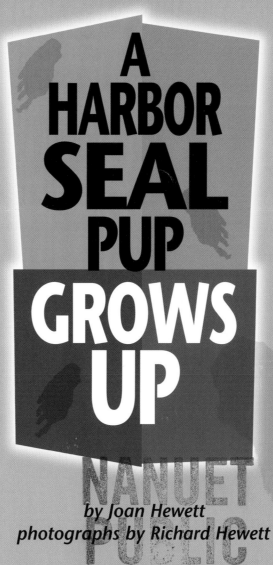

A HARBOR SEAL PUP GROWS UP

GROWS UP

by Joan Hewett

photographs by Richard Hewett

NANUET PUBLIC LIBRARY

CAROLRHODA BOOKS, INC./MINNEAPOLIS

By the Ocean

The harbor seal pup is 2 weeks old.

Her name is Sidney.

Sidney stays close to her mother.

She drinks her mother's milk.

Waves crash on the rocky beach.

Harbor seal families lie in the warm sun.

Sidney and her mother lie in the sun too.

Sidney's mother gets hungry.

She dives in the water to catch fish.

The water is too cold for Sidney.

So Sidney stays on the shore.

The seal pup waits for her mother.
She waits for 3 days.
She is very hungry.

People notice the seal pup.
She is alone.
Will her mother come back?

The next day, the pup is still alone.
The people call for help.
Sidney is rescued.

Nursed Back to Health

Sidney is brought to a sea mammal center.

A scientist named
Peter is in charge.
Peter takes care
of young seals.
He lifts the thin pup
from her cage.

Sidney is weak from hunger.
Peter knows just what to do.
He puts a tube in Sidney's mouth.

Then Nicole pumps a drink
into Sidney's stomach.
The drink is like
a mother seal's milk.

Sidney is full.
She is also very tired.
She falls asleep.

When Sidney wakes up,
her eyes are bright.
She looks around.

Peter examines the pup.
Her heartbeat is normal.
So is her temperature.
She is healthy.

Sidney has a full set of teeth.
That means she is at least 3 weeks old.
Sidney is small for her age.

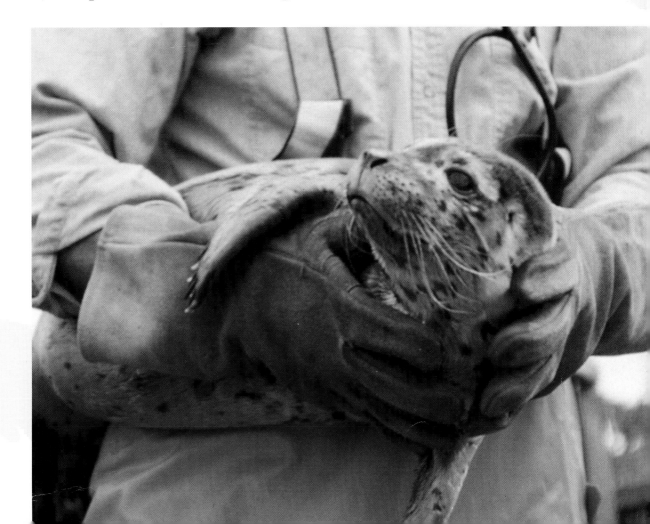

Sidney gets her drink 3 times a day.
She becomes stronger.
Using her flippers, she scoots around.

A child's plastic pool
becomes Sidney's playpen.
She likes the water.
She swims faster and faster.

Nicole shows Sidney
a fish.
Sidney does not want it.

Nicole does not give up.
Day after day,
she wiggles a fish in front of Sidney.
Then one day, the pup swallows it.

Before long, Sidney wants to eat fish.
She waits for her bucket of fish
in the morning.

The pup is gaining weight.

She no longer needs her healthy drink.

Sidney is 5 weeks old.

She has a thick layer of fat.

The fat will keep her warm in cold water.

Sidney is ready to be on her own.

NANUET PUBLIC LIBRARY
149 Church Street
Nanuet, New York 10954

RETURNING TO THE OCEAN

Peter puts the pup in a carrying case.

Other scientists take over.

They carry Sidney onto a boat.

Sidney is excited

by the ocean's salty smell.

She shakes the case.

The boat heads toward an island.
When they are almost there, the boat stops.
It is time to say good-bye.

A scientist tips the case.

"Good luck, little one," she says.

Sidney slips into the water.

She will find other seals.

She will catch fish.

Sidney will grow up in her ocean home.

Sidney
drinks her
mother's milk.

Sidney's mother
goes to fish
in the ocean.

More about Harbor Seals

Harbor Seals are marine mammals. The ocean is their home. Yet, like mammals that live on land, harbor seals nurse their young with milk from their own bodies.

Sidney was born in a harbor seal rookery. A seal rookery is a place where seals gather to give birth and nurse their pups. Each year, a mother seal gives birth to one pup.

When mother harbor seals go fishing, they leave their pups in the rookery. On their return, mothers and pups call to one another. Then they sniff one another carefully to be sure of each other's identity. A harbor seal mother will only nurse her own pup. So a nursing pup that has no mother will not survive.

Harbor seals are good mothers. So something must have happened to Sidney's mother to keep her from returning.

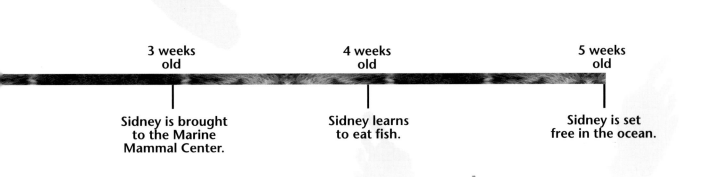

3 weeks old	4 weeks old	5 weeks old
Sidney is brought to the Marine Mammal Center.	Sidney learns to eat fish.	Sidney is set free in the ocean.

Rescuing Orphaned Harbor Seal Pups

In southern California, harbor seal pups are born from mid-winter through spring. This is called the pupping season. During pupping season, people from a group called Seal Watch patrol some of the rookeries. They look for pups that have no mother.

When Seal Watch was sure Sidney was orphaned, they called Peter Howorth. Peter is the director of the Santa Barbara Marine Mammal Center. Each pupping season, he cares for 10 to 20 orphaned harbor seal pups. Most are successfully nursed back to health. Seal pups like to be played with, but Peter makes sure that they do not get too much attention. Seals are wild animals. They don't make good pets. When the seal pups are healthy and strong enough, Peter returns them to their life in the ocean.

Sidney was set free near a group of islands called Channel Island National Park. Thousands of harbor seals swim in the clear water and sun themselves on the islands' peaceful rocky shores.

To Orson Ridgely Hewett, our first grandchild

Text copyright © 2002 by Joan Hewett
Photographs copyright © 2002 by Richard Hewett

All rights reserved. International copyright secured. No part of this book may be reproduced, stored in a retrieval system, or transmitted in any form or by any means—electronic, mechanical, photocopying, recording, or otherwise—without the prior written permission of Carolrhoda Books, Inc., except for brief quotations in an acknowledged review.

This book is available in two editions:
Library binding by Carolrhoda Books, Inc.,
  a division of Lerner Publishing Group
Soft cover by First Avenue Editions,
  an imprint of Lerner Publishing Group
241 First Avenue North
Minneapolis, MN 55401 U.S.A.

Website address: www.lernerbooks.com

Library of Congress Cataloging-in-Publication Data

Hewett, Joan.
  A harbor seal pup grows up / by Joan Hewett ; photographs by Richard Hewett.
      p.   cm.
    ISBN 1-57505-166-4 (lib. bdg. : alk. paper)
    ISBN 0-8225-0092-2 (pbk. : alk. paper)
    1. Harbor seal—Infancy—Juvenile literature. [1. Harbor seal. 2. Seals (Animals) 3. Animals—Infancy. 4. Wildlife rescue.] I. Hewett, Richard, ill. II. Title.
  QL737.P64 H484 2002
  599.79′23—dc21   00-011446

Manufactured in the United States of America
1 2 3 4 5 6 – JR – 07 06 05 04 03 02